The
10 Week
Wedding Planner

How to plan your wedding

in just ten weeks,

how we did it &

how you can too!

Jen Carter
&
Alissa Evelyn

DEDICATION

To everyone who helped us to make
Pete & Alissa's wedding day so special,
you know who you are,
we really couldn't have done it without you!

CONTENTS

OUR STORY

"Mum, Pete just asked me to marry him! .... we'd like to get married soon, maybe October?"

It was already July – this would give us less than three months to plan an entire wedding. In fact, just a mere ten weeks away …

10 weeks?

Was my daughter completely crazy?!

Just a few months earlier my daughter, Alissa, had returned from a summer in Australia. We've always been such good friends and enjoy spending our time together, talking, walking and planning. One day in November, Alissa returned from an evening out, bubbling and excited, saying she'd met a really lovely guy who seemed too good to be true. Even better news, she thought that he liked her just as much as she liked him.

The very next day Pete got in touch and invited Alissa out on a date. Boy, were we excited! One week later our faces beamed as we saw his gleaming black Audi pull up in front of the house to pick her up - it was a scene that Jane Austen herself would have dreamed up if she lived in modern day England.

It was a fairy tale romance, beautiful dates over dinner, romantic kisses on dark evenings and love blossoming as they grew to know each other. They spent almost every evening and weekend that they could together and when they couldn't be together, they were always talking on the phone.

It was quickly clear that these two were going to be together forever, they were so totally in love and seemed to have been made for each other. It seemed only a matter of time until Pete popped the question.

It was no great surprise to me to hear that Pete was planning to ask Alissa to marry him - he was even smart enough to ask for my thoughts on his plans to ask her - what wasn't to love about this guy?!

On Friday July 13th, just eight months after they first met, Pete took Alissa for a special birthday day out, a day filled with romantic gestures that climaxed with him getting down on one knee to ask her to marry him in a restaurant. Her positive response was greeted by rapturous applause from everyone in the crowded restaurant.

It wasn't long after that I had an excited phone call from Alissa to let me know she was going to be marrying the man of her dreams!

As everyone congratulated them, the very next question they asked was "So, when is the big day?". Alissa and Pete knew they wanted a short engagement, and had originally thought of getting married the following year.

However, one day it occurred to them both to ask the question, "Why can't we get married sooner?". As they discussed it, one particular date seemed to come for the fore.

This was a date in October when Alissa's great aunt would be over from Australia and they had already booked time off work to spend a week together.

So it was decided, on Monday 23rd of July, we set a provisional wedding date of Saturday 6th October, just under 10 weeks away.

With Alissa's words, 'Mum, we'd like to get married very soon, maybe October?" still ringing in my ears, I felt like the world I knew was disappearing and that I was walking, or perhaps falling, into the unknown.

Not only did I have a wedding to plan, but I had to do it whilst knowing that I was losing my lovely daughter even sooner than I had thought. We had shared so much together, good times of holidays, movies and countryside walks, health challenges, special moments and times of disappointments, and now all this was seemingly ending.

My daughter was getting married, my world was about to change forever …

HELP, I'M OVERWHELMED!

So I did what any reasonable, sensible mum would do ....
buried my head in the sand and pretended it wasn't
happening! After all, most people I knew took several
months, even years, to plan a wedding, not just a few weeks.

My head was in complete overload, my heart was in denial
and I had absolutely **NO IDEA** whether it was *even possible*
to plan a wedding in such a short time.

In short, I was a mess! Pete, Alissa and myself all had busy,
full-time jobs, how on earth could we plan a wedding?!

When I spoke with friends, their response was disbelief and
incredulity that we were even considering this hair-brained
idea!

One day I woke up and decided that enough was enough. I
could not bear feeling this anxious and disorganised.

There were so many things to be agreed and sorted before we could confirm this date, but we were ON, there was a wedding to plan, and just ten weeks to plan it in. It was time to get organised!

What I'd do was to put together a plan, that would *either* prove that we could put together the wedding of Alissa's dreams in under 10 weeks, *or* give me the ammunition I needed to prove to them both that their dream was a crazy impossibility.

So, I grabbed a pen and started writing ... and writing ... and reading, taking notes ... and writing ... the result was THE PLAN.

At the end of the day I had come to a conclusion, it WAS possible to plan a wedding in such a short space of time .... but only if we were very organised and stuck with THE PLAN.

This meant that there were to be no distractions, diversions or deviations, just a simple following of THE PLAN we had made.

Hooray! Finally, there was light at the end of the tunnel - I went from feeling overwhelmed to organised, we had ourselves a wedding to get ready for.

Was It Worth It?

It's nearly a year since the wedding and people still comment on what a lovely wedding it was. Pete and Alissa are loving their married life together.

"Even after so many weeks and months have passed, friends and family still talk about the wedding and say just how special and perfect everything was. Amazing, considering that it was all planned in just ten short weeks!" Jen

I now believe that almost anything is possible, if you set your mind to it, get the right tools and get organised. We learned so much about what was possible, where we had to compromise and discovered we could even enjoy the whirlwind journey towards their wedding day.

A few days after the wedding, as I enjoyed a well-earned break in the south of France, I asked myself the question, was it worth it? After a manic few weeks, *if I knew everything then that I know now, would I do it again?*

The answer was an unequivocal 'Yes'! The radiant joy on my daughters face as she married the man of her dreams said it all - yes, it was all worth it.

Is planning a wedding from start to finish in such a short space of time for everyone? Most certainly not!

This guide aims to help you decide whether planning a wedding in 10 weeks could work for you. If you feel that it is, then feel free to use and adapt my "10 week wedding planning guide" which is the actual plan that we worked from for those crazy, hectic weeks.

The guide is deliberately compact and concise, as if you have only a few weeks to plan your wedding, you won't have a week to read the 'how to' guide! We have written this so that you can read everything you need to in 30 minutes or less.

Our focus is to help you focus and to **GET STUFF DONE**. So we are not wasting time with stuff that fills up pages but doesn't help you, you'll find not time-wasting stuff here.

Hopefully, reading this book will save you the pain and heartache of finding out the tough way that a 10 week wedding is not for you.

BEFORE YOU TAKE THE FIRST STEP

What we quickly discovered on our wedding planning journey is that we were taking the same steps as every bride that has gone before us, from choosing the perfect dress and shoes, to picking out flowers, cakes and vows.

However, whereas most brides have months, or years, to spend picking out their venue, we had a packed diary for ten weeks after which we could put our feet up for a well-earned rest!

If you think about the way most weddings are planned, there's a few weeks of busy organising, then a period of several months where there's very little that needs to happen, until the few weeks leading up to the wedding when the pace picks up again.

All we have done in the **Ten Week Wedding Planner** is to miss out those months where you're sat kicking your heels eagerly awaiting your special day and done away with all that tedious and impossible waiting!

Planning a wedding in short space of time really builds momentum, focuses the mind and can be an exciting and fulfilling time for everyone involved.

But planning a wedding in such a short time really is NOT for everyone.

Read our checklist in the next chapter 'Could It Work For You' to see whether you are ready to take on the challenge of the Ten Week Wedding.

COULD IT WORK FOR YOU?

It's important to emphasise that planning a wedding in 10 weeks isn't for everybody.

If you've been dreaming of and planning your wedding since you were a little girl, have scrapbooks full of pictures of how you would like your special day to be, and have your mind set on a bespoke designer gown, you will have to have a very strong reason to get married quickly.

If, however, all you want is to be married to the man of your dreams, and that's more important than every tiny detail of your wedding day, then maybe, *just maybe*, this could work for you.

The reality is, *it might not work for you.* The simple 10 point checklist *below* could save you the heartache of trying, and failing, to plan your wedding in just a few weeks.

To see whether it could work for you, check whether you agree or disagree with the ten statements below.

10 Point Checklist

Do you agree that ...

1. The bride, groom and mother of the bride are all able and happy to compromise from time to time

2. We have funds in place for the type of wedding that we want

3. We know friends, family or work colleagues who can help out when needed

4. We are certain we want to get married, with absolutely no doubts about us being right for each other

5. I don't get stressed easily and am usually a fairly calm person

6. I am able to talk and discuss things easily with my future husband

7. We are not planning to get married at the very busiest time of year

8. I have some free time during the evenings and at weekends to plan a wedding

9. I am able to make decisions quickly, when needed

10. My parents, my friends, my future spouse or I, have good organisational skills

Now total up how many you agree with and how many you disagree with.

If you disagree with three or more of these statements, it's highly likely that the Ten Week Wedding Plan is not for you at this point in time. If this is you, use this as a discussion point, to see if it can help you solve or remove any of these stumbling blocks you identified.

If you agree with most of these statements, you have a good chance of being able to make this work.

When planning such a big event in a short space of time, you'll find that everything will be done 'just in time', but not before. It does work, we proved it, others have before us and you can to - but you need to be honest with yourself.

YOUR FIRST STEP

If you're reading this page, I guess that you've decided to explore further how you could plan your dream wedding in just a few weeks.

Of the many things we learnt on our own journey, I'm just about to share one of the most important with you - let's call it 'the two things'.

The Two Things

Before you start your journey towards your big day, both the bride and the groom should each choose TWO things that are key and important to them about your wedding day.

It's likely that you've spent some time thinking how your wedding day will look. Maybe you've even been thinking about the perfect wedding since you were a little girl. When working with such a short time span, you won't have time to get every tiny detail exactly the way you want it, but you can decide on the two dream things that you absolutely refuse to compromise on.

For example, the bride might say that it's the gown and reception venue, the bridegroom might say that it's his bachelor party (or stag night, bull's party or buck's night, depending on where you live) and the food.

"My dream was that the venue looked really pretty, with twinkling lights, just as I had always imagined it to be. I also wanted every guest to be able to come to both the wedding and the reception. For Pete, it was important to have all his friends present and to ensure that all the guests had a really enjoyable day." Alissa - bride

You may also need to take into account the thoughts of any parents who are significantly involved in the planning or funding of your big day - but remember, each person only gets to choose two things.

"Alissa already had her dream man, so my two things were to give her kind of unique day that reflected her style and taste, and to do everything within our limited budget, without going into debt" Jen – mother of the bride

Once each person has chosen their two things - you will need to be willing to compromise on everything else, and perhaps make a few small sacrifices on the way. However in your TWO things, you are allowed to put your foot down and hold out for something close to your dream.

This can be really helpful when you are disagreeing about something in the plan. If it's not on your list of TWO things, and it's not on his list either, then BOTH of you will need to choose to consider a compromise and to make a quick decision.

If it is on your list, or his, then take a little longer to try and find something that meets your dreams or aspirations, and allow for this when you are creating your own week-by-week wedding planning checklist by moving them into the first four weeks of the plan.

A plea to parents - especially the mother of the bride – your dreams of your daughter's perfect wedding day *may not* be the same as her dreams. Remember that this is HER special day, not yours. It's time to let go of your dreams for her wedding day and do everything in your power to help make her dreams come true.

"As we tried on wedding dresses, there was one in particular that I absolutely loved, Alissa looked like a princess, yet she preferred another dress. However, the one I loved was over budget, and as we reviewed all the photos of Alissa in different dresses even I had to admit that it was the dress she had chosen that made her smile and look like a radiant bride.

As I reflected, I remembered that my two rules were to come in within budget and for the wedding day to reflect Alissa's taste and style (not mine). Time for me to let go, again."

Accept All Offers

Whilst some people will be incredulous at what you are planning to achieve, others will offer to help.

Accept every offer of help - make a note of who has offered help, and what they can help with. It's also helpful when saying thank you to all the right people, once your special day has happened and you have a few minutes to relax and breathe again.

If you're feeling uncomfortable about people helping out, ask yourself why. Wouldn't you want to help a friend or family member with their special day? People love weddings and love being involved in the magic of the day - why not share the joy by accepting their offer of help?

We found that almost everyone we asked was happy to help in some way – whether that was in offering flowers from their garden, catering, setting up the venue – everything we needed to make the day such a memorable one.

THE RULES OF THE GAME

So, the game is on!

If you are to keep your sanity over the next few precious weeks, there's a few things you really need to know and remember.

Follow The Plan

With so much to do in so little time, it's essential you follow a plan. Of course, if there's an opportunity to get something done earlier, you can do it, but only if there's time and preferably by swapping with something else that can wait until later.

It'll be tempting to do 'just' one more thing - but if you are happy with your plan, then stick to it.

Resist the temptation to do just one more thing this week. *Believe in the plan* and you will arrive at the Wedding Day with everything organised and in place!

Learn To Love Lists

Lists can save you time and anxiety. If it's on a list, you don't need to worry about it, it will get taken care of, either by you or by someone else.

Get used to creating lists and checklists - for the venue, the caterers, the week before the wedding - and keep them all in one place, or print them out and carry them with you ('the wedding folder", see later), if you prefer.

Use technology to your advantage, create lists on your computer, notebook, ipad, or phone. You could use Dropbox, iCloud or Google docs to allow easy sharing and updating of key information. Update these lists regularly, print out and refer to them often.

"In all the bustle, my brain turned to mush. Each time this happened I could go back to my list - instead of hundreds of things to do, now all I had was one thing to do, whatever was 'the next thing on the list'!

So don't be afraid to use a few sheets of paper or a notepad, write or scrawl all over them - find what works for you, update it regularly and keep a copy with you.

Ignore Everyone Else

Most people won't understand what you are doing. Even your best friends will sometimes question your sanity.

So-called friends will be very willing to give you advice of what you should be doing, tell you what you're doing wrong, or what you should have already done weeks ago!

Others will panic that you haven't sorted out the invitations yet, or that you aren't even planning to THINK about creating a table plan until two weeks before the wedding, but this is YOUR wedding, not theirs and you're entitled to make your own decisions about what to do when.

Surprisingly, you may even face probing questions and even criticism from people you thought were on your side.

"You're mad! Are you telling me that it's four weeks before the wedding and they haven't even bought their wedding rings yet?!" *- yes, this was the kind of 'helpful' conversation family chose to have with myself as mother of the bride. They thought they were*

being helpful, but in reality all they did was add to my stress. I
quickly found a way of 'listening' to them, but not taking on board
anything they were saying ... or changing the subject quickly ... it
was the only way I could retain my sanity." Jen

Ignore them all! (Unless they've planned a wedding in 10 weeks, in which case, buy them a coffee and soak up their advice.)

You have a plan and if you stick to it, you and your dream team will show them all that it CAN be done. In just a few weeks, you will be married to the man of your dreams and this will all be history!

Communicate!

It's essential that you communicate about all the decisions, whether large or small, to ensure that those who need to know are aware of what is happening and that they're happy with it.

There's no time for last minute panics or changes of mind, as are common in weddings where the planning takes months or years. Once a decision is made, unless it's something on your list of two things or his, forget about it and move on.

Use The Power Of The Domino Effect

If you've ever played with dominos, you might have played the game of standing them all up and seeing the knock-on effect of pushing just one domino over.

It's rather like planning a wedding in ten weeks, everything needs to be lined up, in order, so that everything can go smoothly. One thing impacts another.

For example, the guest list needs to be finalised before you can send out invitations or agree numbers for catering. You can move some things around in the plan, but others will need to be thought through as they impact other items on the checklist later in the timeline, so must be done early on.

As you write out your list, bear this in mind to ensure that everything flows well and in the right order.

Book In Personal Time

With everything needing to happen quickly, it can feel like you're being swept along with little time for each other. So plan to book in some special time together, as without this it can all get too much and you may find yourself in emotional overload.

Even with all this preparation, there may come moments, especially for the bride-to-be, where it all seems too much. Expect a few emotional upsets, a few tears from time to time in the weeks before a wedding are normal.

It's SO important to put in the diary *at least once every fortnight,* a relaxing evening or date night when you can just spend time being with your future husband, enjoy time together and remember why it is you want to be together forever.

Create A Wedding Folder

Surprisingly a wedding creates a lot of paperwork - booking forms, emails, photos, and so much more.

Put all this information together in one folder so you know where every piece of paper is. This can be helpful for everyone who's helping you, as they know where to go to find anything relating to the wedding planning.

"Had we paid the deposit for the venue? A quick look at the wedding folder and I found the receipt for the deposit, together with a note of the final amount we needed to pay and when we needed to pay it. Phew, disaster averted once again!" Jen

Put Together Your Dream Team

Whether you're usually a loner, or prefer to work in a team, this is one time where you simply MUST have a team.

It can be small (eg mum, bridegroom, bridesmaid/maid of honor) and ideally at least one person in the team will need

to have good or excellent organisational skills. Don't be afraid to ask people for help - everyone loves a wedding and most people will be flattered that you've asked them for their assistance and input.

You may feel awkward about asking some people, why not consider asking to help out as their special 'wedding gift' to you - some people will love this idea.

" "I'll help organise the catering team for your daughter's wedding. A friend helped out at my daughters and I'd be happy to help with yours." These words were like a dream come true to me. It went against the grain for me to accept this offer of help, but I knew that I couldn't manage without her, so I happily said a hearty yes" Jen

Once you've started planning, have regular time (in person, or on the phone) with your dream team, this will help enormously when your stress levels start to climb and you have people who you can delegate to or ask for help.

The only times when you may be able to live without a 'dream team' is if you have an absolutely massive budget and can hire in someone to organise everything for you, or when you are not working full-time in the weeks leading up to the wedding.

So, who will you include on your dream team?

Simple Rules

These simple rules above can help you survive the busiest few weeks of your life.

Here's a reminder of them:-

1. Choose the two things that are most important to you on your wedding day
2. Accept all offers
3. Follow the plan
4. Learn to love lists
5. Ignore everyone else
6. Use the power of the Domino Effect
7. Book in personal time
8. Create a wedding folder
9. Put together a Dream Team
10. Follow these rules!

Hopefully by following them you can remain calm and organised, but also enjoy the weeks leading up to your special wedding day.

CREATING YOUR WEDDING PLANNING CHECKLIST

In the final chapter you will find the actual checklist that we used to plan Pete & Alissa's wedding.

This is a great starting point to use when planning your own wedding - every wedding is different, but each one includes the same key elements such as dress, vows, flowers, etc.

The first thing that you need to sort out will be the wedding and reception venues. These are the big building blocks that everything else fits around and will influence your other choices and decisions.

So, start with your 'dominoes' and think: what do you need to include in YOUR plan? Then, using the Week By Week Wedding Planning Checklist in the final chapter, draft out your own plan.

It may look simple, but it worked for us. Following these guidelines saved us many times from feeling overwhelmed by all that had to be done in such a short time.

We found that having a printed copy of the checklist with us at all times was very helpful. This made it easy to add things we thought of and remind ourselves of what needed to be done over the next few days. Why not keep this on your smartphone, computer or iPad, for quick reference?

Whatever works for you, make sure that you have a copy of the checklist to hand at all times!

WHAT ARE YOUR DOMINOES?

As we have already mentioned, in order for your wedding planning to run smoothly, you need to ensure that everything happens in the right order.

Here are a few of the big 'building blocks' or 'dominoes' we used that you may also wish to include in your plan - feel free to add your own - every bride and wedding is different!

DATE

- agree on possible dates
- finalise a date
- send out a 'save the date' to friends and family (using email/social media/phone)

CHURCH OR CEREMONY

- find and book a venue for your wedding ceremony
- register your wedding (or whatever legal requirement is necessary)

- book someone to carry out your ceremony

- choose hymns/songs/music and readings

- create and print order of service

- arrange a car for bride/bridegroom to the ceremony and on to reception venue

RECEPTION VENUE

- find, visit and book a venue

- create table plan

- consider and agree colour theme, if required

- plan decorations

- plan wedding favours

WEDDING DRESS & CLOTHING

- book appointment(s) with bridal stores

- choose clothing for bridegroom, best man, ushers and bridesmaids

GUESTS & ATTENDANTS

- create initial guest list (with input from bride, groom, mothers and fathers of bride and groom)

- agree on number and names of best man, ushers, bridesmaids, maid of honour, etc
- agree on final number of guests
- adjust guest list as necessary to fit venue(s)
- send out invitations and compile final guest list
- chase up guests who haven't replied (social media/texting can be speedy when you're in a hurry)

CATERING
- plan wedding breakfast menu
- plan drinks (types & quantities)
- plan help needed for serving (friends or caterers)
- order wedding cake or make plans for cake (eg asking friend to make or decorate for you)

MONEY
- explore funds available
- create initial budget
- decide who will pay for what (eg parents of the bride or groom, bride, groom, etc)
- revise budget, as needed

- pay for church, reception, dress, cake, clothing hire - note in plan any items that need to be paid ahead of the wedding day
- agree or compile a present/gift list - preferably online as this is easiest to circulate quickly to your guests

FLOWERS

- decide on style/colour of flowers
- plan bridal bouquet, bridesmaid flowers, flowers for ceremony and reception venue, buttonholes and corsages for key guests

OTHER IMPORTANT THINGS TO REMEMBER

- plan the timings of your wedding day - e.g. hair & beauty, time for car to pick you up, arrival time at church, arrival time at reception venue, time of departure of bride and groom
- buy wedding rings
- organise stag and hen events (hint: get someone to plan them for you!)
- book wedding night hotel and honeymoon venue

These are the 'building blocks' or dominoes that we used in planning our wedding.

Once you have created your own list of dominoes, you are ready to move on to create your wedding plan.

THE PLAN

OUR WEEK BY WEEK WEDDING PLAN CHECKLIST

Over the next few pages you will find the exact plan that we used to plan Pete and Alissa's wedding.

Hopefully this can give you ideas so that you can start to create your own personalized checklist.

Week 1

- Decide wedding date & create 'save the date' event on social media (e.g. Facebook, Twitter) to inform friends and family
- Explore options for church & reception venues for 6/10/12
- Shortlist, choose and book venue(s)
- Ask friends & family to be bridesmaids; ditto best men and groomsmen
- Book glass hire
- Create wedding folder
- Mother of the bride to buy her wedding outfit
- Plan date/venues/people/appointments for wedding dress shopping

Week 2

- Wedding invites - decide on wording and organise printing
- Plan quantities & purchase of wedding drinks (wine, champagne & beer)
- Saturday 11th - trying on wedding dresses
- Sort bridesmaids cars
- Book wedding car
- Plan hen/stag parties with best man/bridesmaids
-

Week 3

- Wedding dress shopping or planning to have a dress made

- Trip to sort/buy soft and alcoholic drinks

- Speak with possible team for catering/buffet - friends to

organise, plan catering requirements (ready for invitations)

- Finalise wedding guest list - with addresses

- Wedding Present list or ideas ready to send to guests

- Plan out food - including who brings what and quantities

- Plan timings throughout day

- Pay deposits for church and reception venue

- Explore options re wedding cake & make a plan for who is

making/helping

Week 4

- Groom & others to choose suits and/or ties/cravats or order grooms suit hire etc
- Buy or alter wedding dress
- Plans teams of people to serve - food, washing up, parking cars, set up and take down venue, etc
- Printing wedding invites & post out - send together with 'who brings what', map, gift list, mention that venue is unheated + portable loos, etc
- Complete legal formalities (ie register) for wedding

Week 5

- Groom to book wedding night hotel or similar

- Plan order of service, choose hymns & readings, etc

- First fitting for wedding dress & adjustments

- Plan & order wedding bouquet, bridesmaids flowers & buttonholes

Week 6

- Order table linen hire or make own

- Buy/make napkins and make/plan table decorations

- Full payment & certificate to the church

- 1st draft order of service ready

- Plan clear up and preparation team

Week 7

- Groom to book/plan honeymoon location or wedding night hotel
- Bride and groom to choose wedding rings
- Orders of service printed
- Final dress fitting
- Finalise guest numbers
- Visit venue - confirm layout, what's available, etc (for us, running water; table size & chairs; take measuring tape; take candle & jam jar; ask re rubbish removal)
- Plan thankyou cards

Week 8

- Stag & Hen 'do's this weekend i.e. 21st/22nd September?

- Confirm final numbers for wedding & reception

- Move more of Bride's boxes in to new home

- Orders of service printed & ready

- Create table plan

Week 9

- Buy wedding rings

- Move more of Bride's boxes/kitchen stuff in to new home

- Buy soft drinks

- Confirm church / reception / caterers etc if necessary

- Print direction signs & laminate ready

Final Week

Sunday

- Pick up tea & coffee making stuff (thermopots and water heaters)
- Pick up lights for venue
- Signs for venue + write cheque to venue

Monday

- Last minute preparation
- Guest plan layout
- Plan & buy thank you gifts
- Phone - confirm arrival time etc of hog roast; confirm toilet hire company time of arrival; confirm table and chair hire company re delivery/collection

Tuesday

- Wash and dry all clothes ready for honeymoon
- Take direction signs to venue before Saturday

- Alissa & Jen beauty appointments

- Pick up any beer/drinks/soft drinks

- Pick up & pay for paper cups

- Get spending money for honeymoon

Wednesday

- Confirm everything ready and in place for Saturday

- Bride to pack ready for Saturday

- Bride & groom spending time together

- Pick up fridge from Durrington and take to barn

- Put iceblocks in fridge, ready for use on Saturday

- Pick up cutlery plus any other catering stuff

- Write out labels for guests place settings

- Pick up holiday spending money

- Write list of photos to be taken - circulate/email to photographer(s)

Thursday

- Pick up Groom's suit

- Set up reception venue with furniture

- Buy bin bags for Sunday (each person to take one bag home with them)
- Switch on fridge in barn area
- Wash & polish cake stands and silver servers
- Mother of the bride to pick up hat & have calming coffee
- Final beauty prep - legs, toes, etc

Friday

- 8-9am Waitrose delivery of salads
- Flowers arriving (am)
- Buy quiches from Waitrose
- Decorate wedding reception venue
- Collect Waitrose glasses
- Pick up extra tables, if required
- Wedding rehearsal 6.30pm - set out teas & coffees ready for Sat am
- Collect flowers / thankyou gift flowers

Saturday - Wedding Day

- Have an awesome breakfast (e.g. scrambled egg and salmon)
- Friend picks up food from Sainsbury's (am)
- 10.00-11.30, guests can drop off their food at the reception venue (so that it's not left in hot cars)
- 11.30am - team to open/uncork red wine
- 12 noon - get married
- 2-7pm have an awesome party
- 7pm onwards, bride & groom to leave the party & have an amazing wedding night!
- everyone else - clear away tables, chairs and everything else into rubbish bags
- Give vintage stuff (vases & cake stands), napkins, away to helpers
- Return cutlery in small boxes with blue lids

Sunday (after wedding)

- Return borrowed drinks glasses

- Return hot drinks flasks etc

- Rubbish bags for - plates; recycling glass; boxes for cutlery;

rubbish; label each bag

- Return hired suits/clothes/hats

- Return everything else

-

Finally

TAKE WELL DESERVED REST & LIVE HAPPILY EVER

AFTER ....

Creating Your Plan

Now that you've seen the kind of layout - you can see that it really is just a bullet pointed list of everything you need to do in any one week.

I recommend doing this digitally (e.g. Word or Pages), as this makes it easy to cut, paste and move items around as you realise the domino effect.

Save this somewhere safe - and email it to yourself or someone else - so that you have at least one copy somewhere else, if the worst should happen and your computer crashes.

Now it's time to take your list of 'dominoes' and create your very own wedding planner.

May I wish you all the very best with your wedding planning adventure, may you have a wonderful wedding day.

A HAPPY ENDING

Since Pete and Alissa's wedding day, other couples we know have taken the plunge to organise a wedding in just a few weeks ... we like to think our own story may have helped give them the courage to do it!

Throughout this book, we've showed images of the dresses that Alissa tried on in the journey to find the perfect dress for her special day.   Here's the dress she finally chose:-

FINAL WORD

Thank you for allowing us to share our story with you. We wish you all the very best for your own wedding preparations!

May your own story be blessed and full of joy, as you plan your life together as husband and wife.

ABOUT THE AUTHORS

Alissa Evelyn has a popular YouTube channel,
www.youtube.com/alissaevelyn and blogs at
http://notjustapples.blogspot.com. She is now married to
Pete, works in web design and loves reading blogs about
pretty things.

Jen Carter is a writer and mother of three children, two sons
and one daughter, Alissa. She is also a grandmother. She
loves learning new things every day and enjoys baking. She
has a rather crazy cocker spaniel.

LEGAL & COPYRIGHT NOTICE

automatically terminated upon such breach (whether or not we notify you of termination).

Upon the termination of the licence, you will promptly and irrevocably delete from your computer systems and other electronic devices any copies of the ebook in your possession or control, and will permanently destroy any paper or other copies of the ebook in your possession or control.

(3)   No advice

The information is not advice, and should not be treated as such.

You must not rely on the information in the ebook as an alternative to advice from an appropriately qualified professional.

If you think you may be suffering from any medical condition you should seek immediate medical attention. You should never delay seeking medical advice, disregard medical advice, or discontinue medical treatment because of information in this book.

(4)   Limited Warranties

Whilst we endeavour to ensure that the information in the ebook is correct, we do not warrant or represent its completeness or accuracy.

We do not warrant or represent that the use of the ebook will lead to any particular outcome or result. In particular, we make no warrant of any kind relating to this ebook

To the maximum extent permitted by applicable law and subject to the first paragraph of Section [5] below, we exclude all representations, warranties and conditions relating to this ebook and the use of this ebook.

(5)   Limitations and exclusions of liability

Nothing in this notice will: (i) limit or exclude our or your liability for death or personal injury resulting from negligence; (ii) limit or exclude our or your liability for fraud or fraudulent misrepresentation; (iii) limit any of our or your liabilities in any way that is not permitted under applicable law; or (iv) exclude any of our or your liabilities that may not be excluded under applicable law.

The limitations and exclusions of liability set out in this Section and elsewhere in this notice: (i) are subject to the preceding paragraph; and (ii) govern all liabilities arising under the notice or in relation to the ebook, including liabilities arising in contract, in tort (including negligence) and for breach of statutory duty.

(6)   Trade marks

The registered and unregistered trade marks or service marks in the ebook are the property of their respective owners. Unless stated otherwise, we do not endorse and are not affiliated with any of the holders of any such rights and as such we cannot grant any licence to exercise such rights.]

(7)   Digital rights management

You acknowledge that this ebook is protected by digital rights management technology, and that we may use this technology to enforce the terms of this notice.

(8)   Governing law

This notice shall be governed by and construed in accordance with English law.

Made in the USA
Charleston, SC
02 January 2014